DATE DUE

Jean-Claude Van Damme

Katherine Lawrence

The Rosen Publishing Group, Inc.
New York

*For Dad, who shared his love of words
and taught me to dream*

Published in 2002 by The Rosen Publishing Group, Inc.
29 East 21st Street, New York, NY 10010

Copyright © 2002 by The Rosen Publishing Group, Inc.

First Edition

Library of Congress Cataloging-in-Publication Data

Lawrence, Katherine.
Jean-Claude van Damme / by Katherine Lawrence.
p. cm. — (Martial arts masters)
Includes bibliographical references and index.
ISBN 0-8239-3517-5 (lib. binding)
1. Damme, Jean-Claude van, 1961- —Juvenile literature.
2. Motion picture actors and actresses—Belgium—
Biography—Juvenile literature. 3. Martial artists—
Belgium—Biography—Juvenile literature.
I. Title. II. Series.
PN2708.D36 L39 2002
791.43'028'092—dc21

CSL 540695   3/03   Lib Bk Exp $18.95   2001003615

Manufactured in the United States of America

Table of Contents

Introduction   5

Chapter 1 Nerd No More   9

Chapter 2 The Big Break   19

Chapter 3 Movie After Movie   39

Chapter 4 Personal Battles   81

Filmography   93

Glossary   98

For More Information   100

For Further Reading   106

Index   108

Jean-Claude Van Damme has made more than thirty movies in his seventeen-year career.

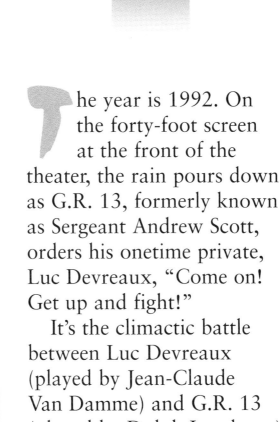

he year is 1992. On the forty-foot screen at the front of the theater, the rain pours down as G.R. 13, formerly known as Sergeant Andrew Scott, orders his onetime private, Luc Devreaux, "Come on! Get up and fight!"

It's the climactic battle between Luc Devreaux (played by Jean-Claude Van Damme) and G.R. 13 (played by Dolph Lundgren) in *Universal Soldier.* The hate has been building steadily between these two men, from the opening scenes in the jungles of Vietnam to this night scene in Louisiana.

Battered by blow after blow, Devreaux lies on the ground and struggles to catch his breath.

Not waiting for a response, G.R. 13 picks up Devreaux and flings him fifteen feet to land face-first in the mud. G.R. 13 is there the moment Devreaux lands, and picks him up again. This time he bashes Devreaux's head into the side of a nearby car.

Finally, disgusted by the lack of response, G.R. 13 throws Devreaux back into the mud. Luc lies there panting from exhaustion. The genetic and chemical cocktail that turned him into a "universal soldier" is breaking him down physically even faster than his opponent.

He hears a cry and looks up to see that the pretty blonde reporter that helped him return home has become the focus of G.R. 13's attention. "Run!" he yells.

She turns to flee, but it's too late. G.R. 13 pulls the pin and throws a grenade toward her. The explosion rocks the wet night.

Devreaux looks up from his prone position. His blood mixes with the rain and mud dripping down his handsome face. The concentration, the courage, the need to win—they're all visible in his eyes as he slowly, painfully pushes himself up off the ground, rising to his feet.

Defying his exhausted body, he runs toward G.R. 13. Without warning he transforms that forward momentum into violence with a high, swinging kick that hits G.R. 13's jaw, rocking the taller man backward and sideways.

Devreaux spins and kicks again and again! He drives his opponent back and back. He pounds him into submission with incredible karate kicks. G.R. 13 doesn't have a chance. The battle is already over; G.R. 13 just doesn't know it yet.

Chapter 1

Nerd No More

Like the character of Luc Devreaux in *Universal Soldier*, Jean-Claude Van Damme has been battered, beaten, and thrown into the mud. Each time, though, he has gathered his courage and determination, and risen to victory.

His original name wasn't Van Damme. He was born Jean-Claude Van Varenberg on October 18, 1960. He originally didn't look like a hero either. When he was young,

Van Damme grew up outside Brussels, Belgium, dreaming of becoming a Hollywood movie star.

Jean-Claude was just like the typical nerd next door—a small, skinny, sensitive kid more interested in painting and classical music than in sports.

"Nerd to your vocabulary, yes," Van Damme says of that time. "I was adorable for my mother."

He had an older sister, Veronique. His dad was a florist and his parents owned their own flower shop. Even worse for a kid with dreams of becoming a movie star, Van Damme was born in Berchem-Sainte-Agathe, outside Brussels, Belgium. This is a very long way from Hollywood. But as Van Damme says, "If you believe in something, it will happen."

He was eleven when his father enrolled him in a Shotokan karate school. In 1971, there were no children's karate classes, so he had to learn with boys sixteen and seventeen years old. He was terrified!

With a determination rare in someone that young, the boy decided he wasn't just going to stop being afraid. He was going to become a karate champion. The young Van Damme worked hard. He practiced day after day. He started weight lifting to increase his strength.

Six years after Van Damme began studying karate, he entered a major three-day championship tournament. For each of those three days, he would wait for his name to be called and have to be immediately ready to fight. There were no age or weight classes, so he was competing with adults far larger and more experienced than himself.

How many bouts did he have? Today, Van Damme doesn't

remember, except that it was around twenty-five when he heard his name again on the third day. His opponent was the man he still considers the toughest person he ever fought.

Jean-Claude felt unable to win even before the match began. This man was the three-time champion and had quite a reputation. Plus, at age twenty-eight, he was eleven years older than Jean-Claude. Jean-Claude tried. He did touch him, but he had already been defeated in his head. He lost the match and his first chance at the championship.

As he said in an *Entertainment Asylum* interview, "So when you believe in something, if you can predict victory, you win already. Don't ever think twice; don't feel like what I felt. But it was a good lesson, because I learned something."

Van Damme took that defeat and learned from it. He earned his black belt in Shotokan karate in 1978. He won the championship before he turned nineteen. That win gave him knowledge of himself that has aided him to this day.

Early Ambitions

Van Damme didn't limit his studies to karate. He also studied ballet, joining the local ballet company. "Every martial artist who's serious should consider taking a few ballet classes. You learn how to stretch much more intelligently and become much more flexible. You also learn how to turn, focus, and so on."

Ballet helped Van Damme focus on movement and position. His ballet interest earned him an offer to join the Paris Opera as a dancer.

He was nicknamed Le Ballon, French for "the Balloon," because he could jump higher from a standing position than anyone else. Van Damme became so good that he was invited to join the Paris Opera as a dancer. He decided instead to focus on karate and weight lifting.

Kickboxing became popular in the 1970s. Van Damme studied the sport.

Determined to be successful, Van Damme opened his own fitness center, the California Gym, in Brussels. He gained his first fame as an entrepreneur and athlete. His interest in the martial arts continued, and he studied Tae Kwon Do, Muay Thai, and kickboxing with champion Dominique Valera.

Then he was given an opportunity that changed his life.

The Wide World

Van Damme had always been fascinated by movies and American television (*Kung Fu* and *The Green*

Hornet in particular). When he was offered the chance to be in the French film *Rue Barbare*, he decided to change his life and pursue acting.

He sold his business, left his family, and went to Hong Kong for the martial arts movie industry. "To leave your family, your friends, your business, and take a chance . . . You've got to believe in your dream."

Work was difficult to come by, however, and in 1981 he decided to go to Hollywood. He had $2,000 in his pocket and didn't speak English. He did have the determination that had earned him his black belt and the karate championship. He was going to make his dream come true.

Chapter 2

The Big Break

Jean-Claude Van Varenberg arrived in Hollywood and promptly changed his surname from Van Varenberg to Van Damme, after a mentor of his from back home. Then he hunted for work.

The next five years were tough. At first he spoke no English and knew no one. Van Damme was forced to sleep in his car for weeks. He also scrounged for food. He took odd jobs, including carpet

Van Damme got his first break in Hollywood with a small role in Chuck Norris's *Missing in Action*.

layer, pizza delivery person, taxi driver, chauffeur, and personal trainer. He began learning English and sought constantly to make new contacts. He talked to producers, directors, actors, and agents.

It was thanks to fellow martial artist Chuck Norris that he got a job as a bouncer in a club. Then he got a small role in the hit movie *Missing in Action,* starring Norris. It was a terrific opportunity, but it was not the big break his career needed.

Missing in Action was followed by tiny parts in *Breakin'* as a passerby during a dance sequence, and in *Monaco Forever,* where his credit reads "Gay Karate Guy."

His next major opportunity for fame came with the role of the kickboxing villain, Ivan, in the low-budget movie *No Retreat, No Surrender* (released as *Karate Tiger* in Europe). Unfortunately, this was a movie only Van Damme fans and those who love cheesy martial arts movies seemed to enjoy.

There are many who dream of fame as a movie star who would have given up at this point. Five years of pounding pavement, lousy jobs, and talking to everyone, and this was his reward?

Then again, as Hollywood screenwriter and novelist Dennis Foley puts it, "The only way to fail in Hollywood is to quit." Jean-Claude Van Damme refused to quit.

It paid off.

During an interview promoting the release of *Universal Soldier: The Return,* when asked how he got discovered, Van Damme said: "I was going to a meeting, to meet some people in a restaurant."

Because he'd done his homework, as Van Damme was entering the restaurant, he recognized a gentleman who was leaving as Menahem Golan, producer of *Revenge of the Ninja* and more than a hundred other action/adventure movies.

"I told him, 'Hey, you should do a film with me. I'm here, I'm young, I'm strong, inexpensive.' And I show him a couple of kicks. I kick above his head; pow! Did a split in the street, and he was like, 'Woh!'"

When Van Damme did this impromptu exhibition of his balletic karate abilities, there were Japanese and Korean film buyers with Golan, and they applauded excitedly. Golan gave Van Damme his card and told Van Damme to come see him.

This was the opportunity he'd been looking for during those five years of struggling to earn the rent, learn English, and memorize who was who in Hollywood. He didn't play the Hollywood game and wait several days before he contacted Golan to avoid looking too eager.

The very next day, he presented himself and the card at Golan's office.

Young actors with few credits, even with such athleticism, good looks, and charm as Van Damme had, are pretty far down the scale of importance in Hollywood. Golan made Van Damme wait, as he remembers it now, for five hours because the producer was busy making deals. "And I was like . . . a slow deal." Finally, he was allowed into Golan's office.

If this were a movie, Golan would have said he had the perfect part for him and handed Van Damme a script. But reality is rarely like that. Golan welcomed Van Damme and asked, "What can I do for you?"

Van Damme was prepared. He knew he had to convince this man to put him in a movie. And not just a movie, but a series of movies, as Golan had done for other action stars, including Chuck Norris.

He'd also done his research and knew the producer's background. Van Damme knew Golan had come to this country from Israel, and had essentially created himself and his career, just like Van Damme hoped to do.

"I'm here to make movies, and I came to this country like you did, and you can take advantage of me. In a good way."

Van Damme did a split between two chairs, now one of his trademark moves, and talked and talked, giving the producer everything he had

Bloodsport was Van Damme's big Hollywood break. He made the splits his signature move.

athletically, intellectually, and emotionally. He wanted to convince Golan that he was exactly what Golan needed for his next movie.

As Van Damme describes the moment, "You have that vision of wanting. You believe in your dream and nothing is happening for days and days and days."

Finally convinced, Golan asked his assistant to bring him the script for *Bloodsport,* for "the kid."

The movie is based on the true story of Frank Dux, the first American winner of the Kumite, an international full-contact martial arts competition. The movie starred Van Damme, along with Donald Gibb (perhaps best known for playing Ogre in the *Revenge of the Nerds* movies), Leah Ayres (guest star on everything from *The A-Team* to *Sliders* after playing a recurring role on *The Edge of Night*), and Forest Whitaker, who went on to win awards and nominations as an actor (*Bird* and *Phenomenon*) and director (*Hope Floats*).

Bloodsport was filmed in Hong Kong for very little money, in Hollywood terms. It cost less than

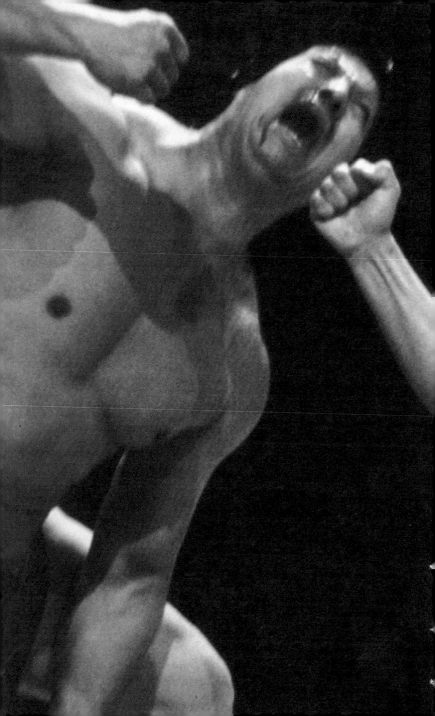

In *Bloodsport*, Van Damme played the role of the first American to win the Kumite.

two million dollars. Unfortunately, according to one story, the low budget showed in the final product. The movie was not released for nearly two years. The story goes on to say that it might never have been released had Van Damme not helped recut the film and begged the producers to release it.

The film went on to earn more than $80 million dollars. That's the equivalent of turning a single dollar into forty dollars, a huge profit by any standard, especially in Hollywood, where movies often cost a small fortune to make. Some even consider *Bloodsport* the best martial arts movie of the twentieth century.

Then again, all was not happy for Van Damme despite the number of people seeing *Bloodsport* at movie theaters. He was nominated for a

Razzie Award by the Golden Raspberry Award Foundation. It gives out awards each year for the worst movie and for the worst acting. (To date, Sylvester Stallone holds the record for the most Razzies won: eight.)

Between the time he was in Hong Kong shooting *Bloodsport* and its eventual release, he never stopped promoting himself and his career. Somehow he instinctively knew that there's no such thing as career momentum in Hollywood.

He took on the role of the alien hunter in *Predator* (1987), which starred Arnold Schwarzenegger, Jesse Ventura—now governor of Minnesota but then known as Jesse "the Body" Ventura, a wrestler with the World Wrestling Federation— and Carl Weathers.

Unfortunately, Van Damme appeared in only one scene. Look for the "hole in the jungle" appearance of the predator. According to *Predator* director John McTiernan (*Die Hard, Last Action Hero*), that's Jean-Claude Van Damme wearing a "blue screen" suit, a special effects suit used to create contrast against the green jungle in the background. After two days of shooting, it was decided that the film needed a taller actor. Van Damme was five feet ten. The studio instead hired Kevin Peter Hall, who was seven feet three.

In addition to hunting down acting work, Van Damme was also tireless about self-promotion. He heard about a swimsuit issue that *Muscle & Fitness*, a bodybuilding magazine, was going to produce. He quickly located the magazine's offices. According to an article in the October 1996 issue, the staff was startled to see Van Damme, then an unknown, and his assistant "come bursting into the office without an appointment."

Van Damme badly wanted to be part of the photo shoot. He showed photos of himself jumping, punching, and kicking to the editor. He also made a point of mentioning a recent European karate contest win.

Unfortunately, there were no seats available on the flight to Cabo San Lucas, Mexico. It was filled with the models, photographer, and staffers. As usual, Van Damme knew what he wanted and kept asking. Finally, he was told, "Well, if you can figure out a way to get down there, it's fine with me, but I won't be able to put you up."

At the end of the first day of shooting on the beach at Cabo, just as the sun was setting, Van Damme and his assistant arrived. With classic Van Damme determination, he'd gotten a flight to La Paz, Bolivia, then "boarded a small plane, flown by some old guy, that had barely made it over the mountains to Cabo."

Soon after he arrived, he spotted one of the bodybuilders modeling swimsuits. He immediately wanted to know who she was and received an introduction. Her name was Gladys Portugues. Later that night he told the editor that he was going to marry her.

Never get in the way of Jean-Claude Van Damme when he makes up his mind about something. Once he has a dream, he makes it come true. He married Portugues that same

Jean-Claude Van Damme and his wife, Gladys Portugues, leave a church in Knokke, Belgium, on June 26, 1999, after they remarried.

year. Though they later divorced, they have since remarried. Van Damme has three children today: Kristopher and Bianca from his marriage to Portugues, and Nicholas from his marriage to Darcy LaPier.

The photo shoot went beautifully, with Van Damme performing his incredible vertical leap into a split. A crew member from *Muscle & Fitness* said, "For an hour and a half, the photographer yells, 'Jump, jump!' over and over. Van Damme is probably five or six feet up in the air in every shot, jumping out of the sand 108 consecutive times . . . and every single shot is perfect!"

Jean-Claude Van Damme performs at the Moulin Rouge in Paris, France, in 1993.

Van Damme proved that day that his combined ballet and martial arts skills showed an athletic grace rarely seen on or off the screen. When added to his accent, good looks, and incredible personal charm and charisma, it was a potent package destined for box office millions.

If his career had ended with the release of *Bloodsport,* he'd have achieved a sizable measure of fame. That would be more than the average guy who comes to Hollywood to become a movie star. But this is Jean-Claude Van Damme. He didn't stop there. His dreams grew.

Chapter 3

Movie After Movie

ollowing *Bloodsport,* Van Damme went on to make a series of action movies: *Black Eagle,* where he again played the villain, *Cyborg, Kickboxer, Lionheart,* and *Death Warrant.*

Each movie took Van Damme a step further along his career path. In *Black Eagle* (1988), an espionage thriller filmed and released before *Bloodsport* hit the theaters, he played his last villain (to date), a Russian named Andrei, opposite Shô Kosugi. *Black Eagle* wasn't a big success. A

Van Damme as Gibson Rickenbacker in *Cyborg*

review by "Fletch-35" on the Internet Movie Database summed it up: "*Black Eagle* could have been a good action movie, if it were given some money to put into the story, which is so bad, after watching the film over ten times, you still don't know what it's about."

That same year he also played a male stripper on the NBC soap opera *Santa Barbara*, with a cast that included Ally Walker, who went on to play the reporter who helped Van Damme in 1992's *Universal Soldier*, as well as later starring in the television series *Profiler*.

In *Cyborg* (1989), Van Damme's first science fiction film, he played Gibson Rickenbacker, a man trying to fulfill a quest in a postapocalyptic world. This film, shot in North Carolina and California, resulted in

In *Kickboxer*, Van Damme plays a cornerman who learns kickboxing to avenge his brother, who was paralyzed by a dirty fighter.

a civil lawsuit from a stuntman who lost vision in one eye after a fight sequence went wrong. It happened during a sword fight, when Van Damme's blade allegedly nicked the stuntman's eye. In the lawsuit, the man claimed that Van Damme was not the expert he claimed to be and lacked the muscle control and training necessary for the stunt. Van Damme lost the lawsuit and had to pay half a million dollars. He swore that for fear of being sued, he would never film in the United States again. However, Van Damme later changed his mind.

Kickboxer (1989) followed and gave Van Damme his first story credit, as well as fight choreographer and fight director credits. He played Kurt Sloane. The movie was so successful it spawned three sequels,

Kurt Sloane (Van Damme) delivers a punishing blow to the once unbeatable Tong Po (Michel Qissi) in *Kickboxer*.

with Sasha Mitchell playing David Sloane, Kurt's younger brother seeking revenge for his big brother's death. There was a fourth sequel that merely used the title.

Next came *Lionheart* (1990)—not to be confused with the historical adventure movie of the same name from 1987—where Van Damme received story credit and shared screenplay credit with the director, in addition to receiving fight choreographer credit and portraying the hero, Lyon. He plays a member of the French foreign legion who deserts when he hears that his brother is in the hospital. The movie was directed by Sheldon Lettich, who wrote other screenplays for Van Damme and went on to direct him a second time in *Double Impact*.

That's one of the fascinating things about Van Damme. He has gained a

In *Lionheart*, Van Damme plays an army deserter who takes part and excels in illegal kickboxing matches to support his sick brother's family.

reputation for being "difficult" to work with, and yet there are a number of writers and directors, as well as actors, who choose to work with him again and again. It speaks well of him and contradicts some of the Hollywood gossip.

Van Damme went from playing a soldier to playing a cop, Louis

Death Warrant is a movie about an undercover policeman (Van Damme, center) investigating the murders of several prison inmates and guards.

Burke, in his next movie, *Death Warrant* (1990). Known for the prison fight scenes, this film shows up a lot on cable television. It also stars Robert Guillaume (*Sports Night*) and Armin Shimerman, the former high school principal on *Buffy the Vampire Slayer* who is also known as Quark on *Deep Space Nine*.

Van Damme's next film stretched his acting muscles as much as his body. With a story by Sheldon Lettich, Jean-Claude Van Damme, Steve Meerson, and Peter Krikes, and a screenplay by Lettich and Van Damme, *Double Impact* (1991) is a tale of twins separated at

Van Damme got to play a dual role—good guy and bad guy—when he starred in *Double Impact*.

birth. One of the brothers is a good guy and the other a bad guy, and the two must join forces to avenge their parents' murder.

In addition to having to be in nearly every scene, often shooting the same scene twice, once as each twin, Van Damme was also producer and fight choreographer.

For female fans, this movie cemented his charm and appeal both as a dangerous, charismatic crook and as a charming, handsome hero. It worked so well he was nominated for a 1992 MTV Movie Award for Most Desirable Male for the double role.

After years of limited film success, Van Damme's breakout movie success came in 1992 with *Universal Soldier*. As mentioned before, the movie starred Van Damme with Dolph Lundgren and Ally Walker, as well as Jerry Orbach (*Law & Order*) and Robert Trebor (*Hercules: The Legendary Journeys*).

Filmed in Arizona and Nevada, the movie was written by Richard Rothstein, Christopher Leitch, and

The good guy/bad guy team of Van Damme and Dolph Lundgren made *Universal Soldier* a fight-fest must-see movie.

Dean Devlin. It was directed by Roland Emmerich. This writing team later brought us *Stargate, Independence Day, Godzilla,* and *The Patriot. Universal Soldier* spawned two made-for-television movies and the feature film *Universal Soldier: The Return* (1999), which also starred Van Damme.

Rosanna Arquette was Van Damme's next costar, in *Nowhere to Run* (1993). As Van Damme said in an interview in *Playgirl* in July 1993, "I'm very surprised for an action star to have so much fan mail from female fans. That's why I did *Nowhere to Run*—just to do something different with more of a story on the love side, the relationship side. I'm trying to please them."

The story credits are impressive: Joe Eszterhas (*Basic Instinct*) and

Nowhere to Run screenwriter Joe Eszterhas answers questions during an interview in Malibu, California, on July 10, 2000.

Richard Marquand (who directed *Star Wars Episode VI: The Return of the Jedi*), with screenplay by Joe Eszterhas, Leslie Bohem (*Dante's Peak, A Nightmare on Elm Street 5: The Dream Child*) and Randy Feldman (*Tango & Cash*). Despite these Hollywood heavy hitters on board, there was more rewriting going on than collaboration. The end result didn't quite work, and the charms of Arquette and Van Damme seemed wasted.

However, in 1993 Van Damme was again nominated for an MTV Movie Award as Most Desirable Male for his role, so obviously there were a lot of very impressed fans.

This was also the first movie where his father, Eugene Van Varenberg, received associate producer credit, which he also received on *Hard Target*, *The Quest*, and *Maximum Risk*.

Then, in 1993, Van Damme played himself in a cameo role in *The Last Action Hero*, which starred Arnold Schwarzenegger. This movie parodied the whole action movie genre, from the never-ending number of bullets

Chinese director John Woo directed his first American movie, *Hard Target*, with help from Van Damme.

in a gun to all those physically impossible heroics.

Later that same year, *Hard Target* was released. This was John Woo's first directing job in the United States. He was brought over from Hong Kong by Van Damme just for this film. Of course, Woo had a flourishing career in Hong Kong, but it was Van Damme who gave him the opportunity to direct his first American movie. *Hard Target* (*Witchblade*) also starred Yancy Butler in her first feature film.

And again, Van Damme received an MTV Movie Award nomination for Most Desirable Male.

That was followed by another science fiction movie: *Timecop* (1994). This worldwide hit movie, filmed in Vancouver, British Columbia, and Pittsburgh, Pennsylvania, costarred Mia Sara and Ron Silver, and led to the spin-off television series of the same name, which starred T. W. King. Incidentally, movie trivia buffs will notice Van Damme take out a stick of "Black Black" Japanese chewing gum while riding in the sled transporting him to the future. In

Colonel Guile (Van Damme) high-kicks General Bison (Raul Julia) during a showdown in *Street Fighter*.

1994, Van Damme also appeared in television commercials for the gum.

Next, Van Damme had some fun. In perfect casting, he played Colonel Guile in both the video game and the movie versions of *Street Fighter* (1994). The movie also starred the late Raul Julia as General M. Bison, the villain, and was written and directed by Steven E. DeSouza (*Die Hard*), who later worked with Van Damme on *Knock Off* as screenwriter.

Sudden Death followed in 1995, directed by Peter Hyams, who also directed Van Damme in *Timecop*. Playing Fire Marshall Darren McCord, Van Damme got a chance to show off his softer side as a family man and father. McCord brings his two children to a hockey playoff game and ends up having to save his children, the vice president of the United States, and the whole stadium

Jean-Claude Van Damme played a family man in *Sudden Death*.

from terrorist Joshua Foss (Powers Boothe), who is threatening to blow everyone up.

Then, in a case of "stunt-casting," Van Damme guest starred as himself on the hit NBC series *Friends* immediately following the 1996 Super Bowl. The episode's title was "The One After the Super Bowl."

In 1994, Van Damme and his son, seven-year-old Kristopher, were guests at the San Diego Comic-Con International. Van Damme discussed a movie he passionately wanted to make: *The Quest*. *The Quest* reached theaters in 1996 and starred Van Damme, his son Kristopher (listed on the credits as Kristopher Van Varenberg), and Roger Moore. Van Damme directed, wrote the story, and cast fifteen of the world's

n Damme assumed total control over *The Quest*. He ote, directed, and starred in the 1996 movie.

Van Damme looks around a Los Angeles courtroom during the trial of a lawsuit that Frank Dux brought against the actor over writing credits for *The Quest*.

greatest martial arts champions as fighters from various countries entering a competition.

There was a controversy over the writing credits, which read "Story by Frank Dux & Jean-Claude Van Damme and Jean-Claude Van Damme, screenplay by Steven Klein and Paul Mones."

What that means by Hollywood and Writers Guild of America rules is that the first draft of the story was written by "Frank Dux & Jean-Claude Van Damme." The second, revised version of the story was written solely by Van Damme. Then Steven Klein wrote the screenplay, and Paul Mones was hired to rewrite the script and rewrote over 50 percent of it.

However, as often happens in Hollywood, the writing credits were

Van Damme and his son Kristopher ride an elephant at Universal Studios' premiere of *The Quest* in Los Angeles, California, in 1996.

disputed. Frank Dux, who was the inspiration for Van Damme's first starring role in *Bloodsport,* had become friends with Van Damme over the years and believed that he deserved greater credit for the film than he received.

This resulted in one of those nasty Hollywood lawsuits. According to an *E! Online* story from September 25, 1997, Dux claimed that Van Damme was "better at ballet than karate and would never have succeeded in movies if [Dux] had not been there to help him." It got nastier, with Dux claiming that Van Damme "should pay punitive damages for misrepresenting himself as a world-class martial artist."

Further, the breach of contract lawsuit claimed Dux cowrote the screenplay that became *The Quest* and that Van Damme cheated him out of a credit and a promised share of the profits. He asked for $1.5 million.

It took more than a year, but in November 1998 a Los Angeles jury ruled 11–1 in Van Damme's favor due to lack of evidence. There was no written contract between Van Damme and Dux.

Unfortunately, *The Quest*, while a solid directorial debut for Van Damme, with an excellent cast that included Roger Moore and James Remar, did poorly at the box office and in online reviews from fans.

The same year that *The Quest* was released, 1996,

Van Damme *(left)* poses with his costars, Janet Gunn and Roger Moore, at the premiere of *The Quest* in 1996.

saw the release of another Van Damme movie: *Maximum Risk*. For this movie, Van Damme brought another Hong Kong action director to U.S. audiences' attention: Ringo Lam. Once again Van Damme plays twins. This time he is a police officer out to avenge his brother's death. He's also being hunted by both the FBI and the Russian Mafia (who mistakes him for the dead twin). The movie costars Natasha Henstridge (*Species*) and Paul Ben-Victor (*The Invisible Man*). Worldwide box office sales exceeded $100 million, a success by anyone's standards.

Then came *Double Team* (1997), which teamed Van Damme up with an unlikely costar, colorful basketball player Dennis Rodman, as counterterrorists out to stop villain Mickey Rourke.

Van Damme in *Double Team* with Dennis Rodman

Dennis Rodman *(center)* arrives at the movie premiere of *Double Team* at Chicago's McClurg Court Cinemas on March 31, 1997.

Audiences clearly didn't accept the movie or the casting. Van Damme and Rodman won the 1998 Razzie Award for Worst Screen Couple, while the movie grossed only $11 million in the United States. By comparison, most of Van Damme's movies do a minimum box office of $30 million.

In 1998, Van Damme starred with Rob Schneider in *Knock Off*, a fun but silly action movie about counterfeit jeans and Russian bombs, with the action choreographed by Sammo Hung, star of the television series *Martial Law*.

Knock Off was followed later in the same year by *Legionnaire*. Filmed in Morocco, it was released direct-to-video in the United States in 1999; this means it never went to U.S. movie houses. In it, Van Damme plays a boxer living the life of a playboy in the 1930s. When he refuses to throw a fight (lose on purpose), he has to run for his life and ends up in the foreign legion.

Legionnaire wasn't a conventional Van Damme action movie in the eyes of the fans and reviewers. But it was nominated for

Playing a 1930s playboy boxer in *Legionnaire*, Van Damme took on a role that stretched his action-hero persona.

an Academy of Science Fiction, Fantasy & Horror Films Saturn Award for Best Genre Home Video Release in 1999, and it was the first film to premiere under the banner of Van Damme's own production company, Long Road.

Then came the cult favorite *Universal Soldier: The Return* (1999), where Van Damme reprised the role of Luc Devreaux. The movie costarred World Champion Wrestling star and former professional football player (Los Angeles Rams and Atlanta Falcons) Bill Goldberg, as well as martial artist Michael Jai White and bodybuilder/fitness trainer Kiana Tom.

When asked what it was like working with Goldberg, Van Damme said he was a "great guy" and liked to do action to the fullest. "I would have to duck, or I wouldn't be here."

Another film produced by his Long Road production company was *Desert Heat* (1999). It was originally filmed under the title *Inferno*, then called *Coyote Moon*, but it airs on television as *Desert Heat*. It was directed by John Avildsen (1977 Academy Award winner for Best Director for *Rocky*), written by Tom O'Rourke, and features a wonderful cast, including Pat Morita, Vincent Schiavelli, Larry Drake, Jaime Presley, Jeff Kober, and Priscilla Pointer.

Desert Heat is a remake of a Japanese film, *Yojimbo*. In *Desert Heat*, Van Damme plays Eddie Lomax, a veteran tired of life, looking to repay an old debt before he dies. When the payment, an antique motorcycle, is stolen, Lomax acquires a reason for living: revenge.

Coming Attractions

In September 2001, *Replicant* was released on video in the United States. It was directed by action movie director Ringo Lam, who also directed Van Damme in *Maximum Risk*. Van Damme once again plays two characters: a serial killer and his genetic clone (a replicant), created to help catch the killer.

In the pipeline following that will be *The Order*, which was directed by Sheldon Lettich, a recurring name in Van Damme's career. It stars Van Damme opposite Charlton Heston, Ben Cross, Sofia Milos, and Brian Thompson. It was supposed to be filmed in Jerusalem and Sofia, Bulgaria, but the Israel shooting time was shortened due to unrest there.

And there's yet another movie in the works for Van Damme. Scheduled

Van Damme dressed as an ultraorthodox Jew during the filming of *The Order* in 2000.

for release in 2002 is *Abominable*. It's currently in production, so things may change, but according to the Internet Movie Database, in this movie Van Damme "plays a park ranger in a remote community where there are sightings of a Big Foot–like creature endangering local residents."

As he's matured, Van Damme has moved past simple action films. His continued work with good writers is sure to thrill audiences for a great many years to come.

Chapter 4

Personal Battles

*D*esert Heat opens with two title cards. The first reads, "In the spring, the full moon shines for the warrior who has lost his way." The second reads, "Coyote is the spirit that leads back to life. If he follows the coyote when the moon is full, the warrior will see the path once more."

This could be considered a metaphor for Jean-Claude Van

Damme's life today as he focuses on new goals.

His personal life has always been filled with ups and downs. At nineteen, he married Maria Rodriguez in Brussels (she was six years older than he was). When he sold his gym and left Brussels for Hong Kong, she was part of the family he left behind, and they separated permanently.

He met Cynthia Derdian when he was still trying to make it in Hollywood, working as a carpet layer for her father. They married in 1985—a marriage that lasted one year.

Next he met bodybuilder Gladys Portugues at the magazine shoot in Cabo San Lucas. Newly divorced from Derdian, Van Damme married Portugues in 1986. Their son,

Van Damme arrives with his wife Darcy LaPier at the Los Angeles premiere of *Sudden Death* on December 14, 1995.

Kristopher, was born in 1987, and their daughter, Bianca, was born in 1990.

But Van Damme and Portugues divorced in 1994 when Van Damme met Darcy LaPier, a Hawaiian Tropic beauty-contest winner. As Van Damme said, "I love Hollywood, but I fell into the trapping of stardom."

Van Damme married LaPier in 1994. Their son, Nicholas, was born in October 1995.

In early December 1996, Van Damme entered a thirty-day substance abuse program in Los Angeles for what was later revealed as a cocaine addiction. He was quoted as saying, "I feel I've been a role model to children . . . and couldn't live with myself if I didn't regain my health and conquer this thing."

He checked himself out with the doctors' permission a week later to be with his children for Christmas, just as his wife filed for divorce.

The following month was filled with tabloid headlines as accusations and counter accusations were made in public and in the courts between Van Damme and LaPier. Despite all this, they reconciled.

In April 1997, Van Damme was quoted as saying, "I did twenty movies. I became a machine." He added, "I did all those action scenes when I was sick," referring to his drug abuse, which included sleeping pills.

Then, in December 1997, his relationship with LaPier hit the headlines again. She filed for divorce from him for the third time, this time claiming that Van Damme regularly beat her and that he suffered from mood swings as a result of his cocaine addiction.

"Van Damme has a voracious cocaine habit. He is also manic-depressive. His mood swings and resulting behavior are horrifying," LaPier said in legal documents filed with the court.

In a *Dateline* interview in 1998, Van Damme denied ever punching, kicking, or throwing his wife to the ground. But he admitted that he had been recently diagnosed with bipolar disorder, sometimes termed manic depression. His mood swings were the result of a chemical imbalance in the brain and had occurred since he was a teenager. He is currently on drug therapy for the problem.

Van Damme and LaPier didn't reconcile. In January 1998, it was reported that Van Damme was going to have to pay $27,000 a month in temporary child support and $85,000 a month in temporary spousal support to keep her in the manner to which she had become accustomed. That's more than $1.3 million a year!

Van Damme continued to hit the tabloid headlines, next for being a participant in an alleged barroom brawl with a former bodyguard of actor Mickey Rourke.

Then, in August of 1998, he talked to the media again about his cocaine addiction, this time in *Entertainment Weekly*. When speaking about the shooting of *Knock Off,* which finished filming in August 1997 in Hong Kong, he said, "I almost passed out . . . I was dying. I saw my body on the floor. I felt cold, I felt hot, I felt scared." However, he added that he went cold turkey, quitting the drugs completely after entering rehab at the end of 1997.

He has his faith to thank for kicking the drug habit. "I believe in God big time. I come back very strong and decent. I'm going to do my best to be a good person."

Next came the decision to rebuild his life. He returned to serious workouts, got back in shape, and returned to Gladys Portugues and their two children, Kristopher and Bianca. Van Damme says of her, "She's my best friend and my soulmate." They remarried in June 1999.

Despite the best of intentions, things still sometimes went wrong. In September 1999, Van Damme was arrested on suspicion of drunken driving in West Hollywood. He first pled not guilty, but changed his mind, pleading no contest.

The following July, he was sentenced to three years' probation and fined $1,200

Van Damme enters an automobile following his release from a Los Angeles County Sheriff's substation in West Hollywood, California, on September 23, 1999. He had been arrested for drunken driving.

for the misdemeanor charges of drunken driving and driving without a license. He was also ordered into a ninety-day alcohol-education program and told he was allowed to drive only to and from work, and to and from the education program.

But that seems to be the last of Van Damme's personal mistakes. At the Cannes Film Festival in 2000, where he was promoting his newest movie, *Replicant*, he said, "The most difficult achievement in life is to be at peace with yourself."

He's turning his life around, day by day.

Of the "new" Van Damme, director Ringo Lam says, "He's got this larger-than-life quality about him. And he's a hero. Some people are just born to be heroes. Had he lived in an earlier age, he would

have been like, Sir Lancelot. He
would have been a knight, or a
centurion, or a crusader, or
something like that. He just has that
quality about him. And in this
modern world, people like that end
up becoming movie stars, I guess.
There's no more dragons to slay,
you know?"

That doesn't keep Van Damme
from finding new dragons to fight,
however. He was part of the People
for the Ethical Treatment of Animals
(PETA) campaign to save thousands
of stray dogs on the streets of Taiwan
by convincing the Taiwanese Premier
to ensure the passage of the animal
protection law, the first in Taiwan.

He has also been a participant in
the Make-A-Wish Foundation.

"You have to become a decent
guy to do decent stuff in life. All I'm

saying to you—what I'm trying to tell you is—I grew up. I start at the age of one to the age of 37. I'm learning every day to become a better man."

If anyone can beat the addictions and turn his or her life around, it's Jean-Claude Van Damme. *No Retreat, No Surrender* isn't just a movie for him, it's a lifestyle.

Filmography

Rue Barbare (1984)

Missing in Action (1984)
stunt performer

Breakin' (1984)
uncredited passerby
during dance sequence

Monaco Forever (1984)
"Gay Karate Guy"

No Retreat, No Surrender (1985)
"Ivan"

Predator (1987)
"alien hunter"

Jean-Claude Van Damme

Bloodsport (1988)
"Frank Dux"

Black Eagle (1988)
"Andrei"

Cyborg (1989)
"Gibson Rickenbacker"

Kickboxer (1989)
"Kurt Sloane," plus story, fight
choreographer, fight director

Lionheart (1990)
"Lyon," plus story and screenplay,
fight choreographer

Death Warrant (1990)
"Louis Burke"

Double Impact (1991)
"Alex" and "Chad," plus story
and screenplay, fight
choreographer, producer

Universal Soldier (1992)
"Luc Devreaux"

Nowhere to Run (1993)
"Sam Gillen"

The Last Action Hero (1993)
cameo role as himself

Hard Target (1993)
"Chance Boudreaux"

Timecop (1994)
"Max Walker"

Street Fighter (1994)
"Colonel Guile"

Street Fighter: The Movie
(videogame, 1994)
"Colonel Guile"

Sudden Death (1995)
"Darren McCord"

The Quest (1996)
"Christopher Dubois,"
plus director, story

Maximum Risk (1996)
"Alain/Mikhail"

Double Team (1997)
"Jack Quinn"

Knock Off (1998)
"Marcus Ray"

Legionnaire (1998)
"Alain Lefevre," plus story

Universal Soldier: The Return (1999)
"Luc Devreaux," plus producer

Coyote Moon aka *Inferno* aka *Desert
Heat* (video title) (1999)
"Eddie Lomax"

Replicant (2001)
"Number One"/"The Torch"

The Order (2001)
"Rudy"

The Monk (2001)
"Monk"

Abominable (2002)

Glossary

charisma   The ability to win people's friendship and trust.

choreographer   The person who designs and controls action or stunt scenes in a movie or play.

director   The person who controls the filming of a movie.

karate   "Empty hands," which means students use their hands and feet as striking weapons.

Muay Thai   A martial art from Thailand, using kicks and punches when attacking.

producer   One who puts up the money
  to make a film, record, or video.
Shotokan karate   A martial art
  devoted to total mind-body control
  to produce precise movements.

For More Information

Associations

In the United States

Advanced Shotokan International
c/o Plattsburgh Karate Club
Box 2032
Plattsburgh, NY 12901
Web site: http://www.netheaven.com/
  ~baldman/asi.html

American JKA Karate Association
3975 Mission Inn Avenue
Riverside, CA 92501
Web site: http://www.americanjka.com

International Shotokan Karate
   Federation
222 South 45th Street
Philadelphia, PA 19104
Web site: http://www.iskf.com

International Traditional Karate
   Federation
1930 Wilshire Boulevard, Suite 1208
Los Angeles, CA 90057
Web site http://www.itkf.org

Shotokan Karate of America
c/o Maryknoll Japanese Catholic Center
222 South Hewitt Street, Room 7
Los Angeles, CA 90012
Web site: http://www.ska.org

Shotokan Karate Association
c/o 52 Manor Drive
Richboro, PA 18954

Shotokan Karate-do America
2121 Broadway, 4th Floor
New York, NY 10023

Shotokan Karate International
Federation-USA
CSUN Martial Arts Center
California State University Northridge
Northridge, CA 91325
Web site: http://www.csun.edu/
~hbcsc302/start.html

USA National Karate-do Federation
P.O. Box 77083
Seattle, WA 98177-7083
Web site: http://www.usankf.org

In Canada

Canadian Chinese Kuo Shu (Martial
Arts) Federation
Woodside Square Postal Outlet
P.O. Box 63517
1571 Sandhurst Circle
Agincourt, ON M1V 1VO
(905) 602-5026
Web site: http://www.wusha.ca

Canadian Chito-Ryu Karate-do
  Association
89 Curlew Avenue
Toronto, ON M3A 2P8
(416) 444-5310
Web site: http://www.chitoryu.ca

Web Sites

Ballet Alert
http://www.balletalert.com
An online newsletter for those who
  enjoy ballet.

E! Online—Fact Sheet—Jean-Claude
Van Damme.
http://www.eonline.com/Facts/People/
  Bio/0,128,131,00.html

Internet Movie Database—Jean-Claude
  Van Damme
http://us.imdb.com/Name?Van+
  Damme,+Jean-Claude

Jean-Claude Van Damme—Official Site
http://www.jcvandamme.net

Mr. Showbiz Celebrities: Jean-Claude
Van Damme Profile
http://mrshowbiz.go.com/celebrities/
people/jeanclaudevandamme/
index.html

National Karate-do Federation
http://www.usankf.org
News, tournament information, and
explanations of the organization,
programs, and membership benefits.

North American Alliance of Martial Arts
http://www.naamakarate.com
An index of schools, teacher bios,
and general descriptions of these
community and family-based
programs.

The Shotokai Encyclopedia—
Karate-do and Martial Arts
http://www.shotokai.com

USA Karate
http://www.usakarate.org
Federation of instructors offers
organizational news, events, rumors,
membership details, and merchandise.

World Karate Federation
http://www.jko.com/wkf.html
Official world body site includes
competition rules, history of the
organization, schedules, and results
from the last world championship.

For Further Reading

Fox, Joe, and Art Michaels. *Kickboxing Basics*. New York: Sterling Publications, 1998.

Funakoshi, Master Gichin. *Karate-Do Kyohan: The Master Text*. New York: Kodansha International Ltd., 1973.

Hassell, Randall. *Shotokan Karate: Its History and Evolution*. St. Louis, MO: Focus Publications, 1998.

Healy, Kevin, and Laura Knox (photographer). *Karate: A Step-by-Step Guide to Shotokan*

Karate. Chicago: NTC/ Contemporary Publishing, 2001.

Meyers, Richard. *Great Martial Arts Movies: From Bruce Lee to Jackie Chan and More*. Secaucus, NJ: Carol Publishing Group, 1999.

Mezger, Guy, et al. *The Complete Idiot's Guide to Kickboxing*. Indianapolis, IN: Alpha Books, 2000.

Rielly, Robin L. *Secrets of Shotokan Karate*. Boston: Charles E. Tuttle Co., 2000.

Sahota, Gursharan. *The Shotokan Karate Handbook: Beginner to Black Belt*. Cincinatti, OH: Seven Hills Book Distributors, 1996.

Sipe, Daniel. *Kickboxing: The Modern Martial Art*. Minneapolis, MN: Capstone Press, 1994.

Umezawa, Rui. *The Empty Hand: A Karate Wordbook*. New York: Weatherhill Press, 1998.

Index

A

Abominable, 80
Arquette, Rosanna, 53, 55

B

ballet, 14–15, 23, 38
Black Eagle, 39–41
Bloodsport, 27–31, 38, 39, 67
Breakin', 21
Brussels, Belgium, 11, 17

C

California Gym, 17
Cyborg, 39, 41–43

D

Death Warrant, 39, 49
Derdian, Cynthia, 82

Desert Heat, 77, 81
Double Impact, 46, 49–51
Double Team, 70–72
Dux, Frank, 27, 67–68

F

Friends, 62

G

Golan, Menahem, 22–27
Goldberg, Bill, 76

H

Hard Target, 55, 56–67
Hong Kong, 18, 27, 31, 56, 70, 82, 87

K

karate, 8, 14, 18, 23, 33

Shotokan karate,
    11, 14
Kickboxer, 39, 43–46
kickboxing, 17
Knock Off, 60, 73, 87

L

Lam, Ringo, 70, 78,
    90–91
LaPier, Darcy, 36, 83–86
Last Action Hero, The,
    55–56
Legionnaire, 73–76
Lionheart, 39, 46
Long Road, 76, 77
Lundgren, Dolph,
    5–8, 51

M

Maximum Risk, 55,
    70, 78
Missing in Action, 21
Monaco Forever, 21
Moore, Roger, 62, 68
MTV Movie Awards,
    51, 55, 57
Muay Thai, 17
Muscle & Fitness
    magazine, 32–36

N

No Retreat, No
    Surrender, 21, 92
Norris, Chuck,
    20–21, 25
Nowhere to Run,
    53–55

O

Order, The, 78

P

Portugues, Gladys,
    34–36, 82, 88
Predator, 31–32

Q

Quest, The, 55, 62–65,
    67–68

R

Razzie Awards,
    31, 72
Replicant, 78, 90
Rodman, Dennis,
    70, 72
Rodriguez, Maria, 82
Rue Barbare, 18

109

S

Santa Barbara, 41
Schwarzenegger,
    Arnold, 31, 55
Street Fighter, 60
Sudden Death, 60–62

T

Tae Kwon Do, 17
Timecop, 57, 60

U

Universal Soldier, 5–8,
    9, 41, 51–53
*Universal Soldier: The
    Return*, 22, 53, 76

V

Valera, Dominique, 17
Van Damme,
    Jean–Claude
    and ballet, 14–15,
        23, 38
    and charities, 91
    childhood, 9–14
    children of, 36, 62,
        82–83, 84, 88
    family of, 11, 18, 36,
        55, 62, 82–84, 88
    in Hollywood, early
        days, 18, 19–32, 38
    and karate, 11–14,
        18, 23, 33
    and lawsuits, 43,
        67–68
    marriages of, 34–36,
        82–84, 88
    movies, 5, 18, 21,
        27, 31, 39–80, 90
    in *Muscle & Fitness*
        magazine, 32–36
    production
        company, 76
    real name, 9, 19
    and substance abuse,
        84–85, 87, 88–90
    television appear-
        ances, 41, 62

W

Walker, Ally, 41, 51
Woo, John, 56–57

About the Author

Katherine Lawrence has had more than thirty television scripts produced, most recently for *X-Men Evolution*, and was nominated for a Writer's Guild of America Award in 1997. She also had four short stories published and is working on her fifth computer game. This is her first book.

She currently lives in Arizona and writes full-time. Her other interests include archery, her sports cars, collecting swords, reading books, and watching action movies. Please visit her at www.katherinelawrence.com

Photo Credits

Cover and pp. 4–5, 20, 26, 28–29, 40, 42, 44–45, 47, 48–49, 50, 52, 58–59, 61, 63, 71, 74–75 © The Everett Collection; p. 10

Series Design and Layout

Les Kanturek